First Facts™

Everyday Character Education

Patience

by **Rebecca Olien**

Consultant:
Madonna Murphy, PhD, Professor of Education
University of St. Francis, Joliet, Illinois
Author, *Character Education in America's Blue Ribbon Schools*

Capstone
press
Mankato, Minnesota

First Facts is published by Capstone Press,
151 Good Counsel Drive, P.O. Box 669, Mankato, Minnesota 56002.
www.capstonepress.com

Library of Congress Cataloging-in-Publication Data
Olien, Rebecca
    Patience / Rebecca Olien.
    p. cm.—(First facts. Everyday character education)
    Summary: "Introduces patience through examples of everyday situations where this character
trait can be used"—Provided by publisher.
    Includes bibliographical references and index.
    ISBN 0-7368-4279-9 (hardcover)
    1. Patience—Juvenile literature. I. Title. II. Series.
BJ1533.P3045 2006
179'.9—dc22   2004026746

Editorial Credits
Becky Viaene, editor; Molly Nei, set designer; Kate Opseth, book designer;
    Wanda Winch, photo researcher/photo editor

Photo Credits
Capstone Press/Karon Dubke, cover, 1, 5, 6, 7, 8–9, 10, 11, 13, 19, 21
Corbis/Bettmann, 17; Geray Sweeney, 20
Leland Bobbe Studio, 14–15

1 2 3 4 5 6 10 09 08 07 06 05

Table of Contents

Patience

Sara is having trouble with a math problem. She doesn't get upset. Instead, Sara raises her hand to ask the teacher for help.

Sara is patient. She waits **calmly** while the teacher helps someone else first. Being patient helps Sara keep trying when learning is hard.

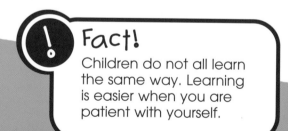

Fact!
Children do not all learn the same way. Learning is easier when you are patient with yourself.

At Your School

Having patience helps you do better in school. You are coloring a picture for art class. You want to color the picture fast.

You are patient and take time to color the picture. Your teacher notices **improvement** from last time. Being patient helped you do a good job.

With Your Friends

Friends are patient with each other. Sometimes it's hard to wait for your turn to talk. Letting your friend finish talking takes patience. Your friend feels good when you listen.

Fact!
Being patient can be fun. You can practice patience by taking turns when you play board games with your friends.

At Home

Patience helps you finish projects. You're helping your dad bake cookies. You set a timer and wait patiently for the cookies to bake.

Your dad takes the cookies out of the oven. You want to eat one, but they are too hot. You and a friend wait patiently for the cookies to cool.

In Your Community

Patience helps you stay safe in your **community**. You and Jeff want to cross the street. The Don't Walk sign is flashing.

You wait patiently for the light to change. You're calm while you wait. When the sign changes to Walk, crossing the street is safe.

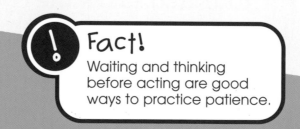

Fact!
Waiting and thinking before acting are good ways to practice patience.

Shifra Mincer

People use patience to help others. Shifra Mincer works patiently to mend clothes. She **sews** clothes for people at a New York City **soup kitchen**.

Shifra began sewing when she was only 10 years old. Since then, she has mended clothes for many people.

Fact!
In 2003, Shifra won the Gloria Barron Prize for Young Heroes.

Thomas Edison

   Patience can help you do great things. Thomas Edison spent months trying to **invent** the lightbulb. Edison failed more than 1,000 times before inventing a working lightbulb in 1879. He had **success** because he was patient.

Fact!
Edison showed a lightbulb to the public for the first time in Menlo Park, New Jersey, on December 31, 1879.

What Would You Do?

Sara's haircut is taking a long time. The chair she is sitting on is starting to feel uncomfortable. Sara wants to get out of the chair. How could Sara show patience while she gets a haircut?

Fact!

One of the fastest-growing parts of the body is hair. But, you need to be patient while it grows. It can take months for hair to grow as long as you want it.

Amazing but True!

Tibetan monks make designs called mandalas out of tiny grains of colored sand. Monks spend days carefully placing the sand in patterns. Soon after the mandala is finished, the sand is swept away. Monks practice patience while making mandalas.

Hands On: Building Patience

You can learn about patience by using playing cards to build a tower.

What You Need

2 friends

1 deck of playing cards

What You Do

1. Work with your friends to build a card tower. Carefully lean two cards so they stand against each other. Now, build a row with two other pairs of standing cards. Place two cards flat on top of the first row. Then build a row of two pairs on top of the first row. Place one card flat on top of the second row. Then build one row on top. What could you do to make it taller?
2. Challenge yourself and your friends to try again.
3. Keep experimenting to build the tallest tower.

Were there times when you needed to use patience? Is it easier to practice patience when working alone or with a friend?

Glossary

calm (KAHM)—quiet and peaceful

community (kuh-MYOO-nuh-tee)—a group of people who live in the same area

improvement (im-PROOV-ment)—to get better, or to make something better

invent (in-VENT)—to think of and make something new; Thomas Edison invented the lightbulb.

sew (SOH)—to make, repair, or fasten something with stitches made by a needle and thread

soup kitchen (SOOP KICH-uhn)—a place that serves prepared food to people who are homeless

success (suhk-SESS)—a good outcome or the results that were hoped for

Read More

Kyle, Kathryn. *Patience.* Wonder Books. Chanhassen, Minn.: Child's World, 2003.

Raatma, Lucia. *Patience.* Character Education. Mankato, Minn.: Bridgestone Books, 2000.

Internet Sites

FactHound offers a safe, fun way to find Internet sites related to this book. All of the sites on FactHound have been researched by our staff.

Here's how:
1. Visit *www.facthound.com*
2. Type in this special code **0736842799** for age-appropriate sites. Or enter a search word related to this book for a more general search.
3. Click on the **Fetch It** button.

FactHound will fetch the best sites for you!

Index